To Daniel, Zach, Ben and Rebekah, who make every breath worth taking. - JSF

To Percy, Gus, Keenie, Hudson, Kip, Ileana, Petal and Tom - the loves of my life. - AGC

And to Mike the magic maker.

Breathe with Todd

A lizard finds peace at bedtime, and so can you.

By Jan Stritzler Fenster and Alex Galfas Carter

Illustrated by Arielle Hadad

ISBN 978-1-09830-153-8

I'm not sleepy!

I'm hungry!

I'm not tired!

Tell me a story!

Sure. We're breathing all the time.
But, there are different ways
to breathe at different times.

Doesn't everyone breathe?

How am I breathing right now?

Breathe on my claw Rebekah, so I can feel
how fast and quick you're breathing.

You are breathing energy breaths.
See how fast they are?

Then what kind of breaths
are you doing Todd?

Mine are sleepy breaths.
See how long and slow they are?

Shhh...

hhh...

hhh...

hhh...

Todd, how did you learn about different ways to breathe?

I learned from my friends. Would you like to meet them?

When you are sleepy breathing, your tummy rises and falls –
just like a wave in the ocean.

When Angus breathes in, his tummy inflates and makes a big wave for me to ride.

And when he breathes out, his tummy goes down, like a wave smoothing out.

This is my friend, Dot.
Her favorite way of sleepy
breathing is in through her nose
and out through her mouth.

First, breathe in through your nose...

...and then out through your mouth.

Shhhhhhhhhhh...

All you have to do is
breathe in through your nose,
and out through your mouth.

You're doing
great Rebekah!

My last friend for you to meet is Tabitha.

She stretches her arms and legs and back while she's sleepy breathing.

It helps her relax.

It feels so good to stretch and sleepy breathe at the same time.

Shhhhhhhhhhh...

I'm sleepy now, it's time for bed.

I close my eyes, and breathe in deep.
I exhale "shhhhhhhhhhh" and fall asleep.

I'm sleepy too.
I yawn and stretch.
It's time for bed.
Sweet dreams, my friends.

Let your happiest, best dreams begin.

About the Authors

Jan started one of the first personal fitness training businesses in New York in 1987. She has an MA from Columbia in Applied Physiology and is certified as a Prana Yoga instructor. Her experience teaching breathing techniques to her own three children, as well as the ones she taught in school, led to this book. Jan currently teaches the power of breathing techniques and posture at Complete Wellness, located in New York City.

Alex traveled extensively while raising her family. Following several years living in both Istanbul and Nicaragua, Alex and her family now call New York City home. Alex is a certified doula and certified yoga instructor. She is the mother of seven children. Her autistic son, Keenie has benefited from the breathing techniques taught in this book.

Arielle Hadad is self-taught New York City based artist, currently perusing a degree in visual arts. Breathe with Todd is her first work as an illustrator, a leap in a new direction from painting and sculpture.

Todd is a real lizard and lives with Alex and her family.